Anonymous

Memorial of the remonstrants, residents and owners of estates in ward XI against the establishment of a new gas light company

Anonymous

Memorial of the remonstrants, residents and owners of estates in ward XI against the establishment of a new gas light company

ISBN/EAN: 9783337269463

Printed in Europe, USA, Canada, Australia, Japan

Cover: Foto ©ninafisch / pixelio.de

More available books at **www.hansebooks.com**

PAMPHLETS.

Gas in Boston, etc

MEMORIAL

OF THE

REMONSTRANTS,

RESIDENTS AND OWNERS OF ESTATES IN WARD XI.

AGAINST THE ESTABLISHMENT

OF A

NEW GAS LIGHT COMPANY,

AT THE SOUTH END.

BOSTON:
1860.
J. H. EASTBURN'S PRESS.

MEMORIAL

OF THE

REMONSTRANTS,

RESIDENTS AND OWNERS OF ESTATES IN WARD XI,

AGAINST THE ESTABLISHMENT

OF A

NEW GAS LIGHT COMPANY,

AT THE SOUTH END.

BOSTON:
1860.
J. H. EASTBURN'S PRESS.

MEMORIAL.

To the Mayor and Board of Aldermen of the City of Boston.

The undersigned, for themselves and the remonstrants against the sale of any of the City Lands at the South End for erecting Gas Works, and against permission being granted to a new Company to open the streets at the South End for the purpose of laying gas pipes, beg leave to lay before you a succinct history of the Suffolk and Shawmut Gas Light Companies, and an accurate account of the hearing before the Committee on Paving, which lately took place, with the evidence then given, and with such other considerations as may be pertinent to the question now or soon to come before your Board for action.

In 1850 a charter was granted to Philo Sanford, Edward F. Hall, Watson Freeman, their associates and successors, incorporating them as the Suffolk Gas Company.

The Act is as follows :

Be it enacted by the Senate and House of Representatives, in General Court assembled, and by the authority of the same, as follows:

SECT. 1. Philo Sanford, Edward F. Hall, Watson Freeman, their associates and successors, are hereby made a Corporation, by the name of the Suffolk Gas Company, for the purpose of manufacturing and selling gas in the Cities of Boston and Roxbury ; with all the powers and privileges, and subject to all the duties, restrictions, and liabilities, set forth in the thirty-eighth and forty-fourth chapters of the Revised Statutes.

SECT. 2. Said Corporation may for the purpose aforesaid, hold real estate not exceeding in value two hundred thousand dollars, and the whole capital stock shall not exceed five hundred thousand dollars.

SECT. 3. Said Corporation shall have power and authority to open the ground in any part of the streets, lanes, and highways, in either of said Cities, with the consent of the Mayor and Aldermen thereof, for the purpose of sinking and repairing such pipes and conductors as it may be necessary to sink for the purpose aforesaid; and the said Corporation after opening the ground in said streets, lanes, and highways, shall be held to put the same into repair, under the penalty of being prosecuted for a nuisance : *provided*, that the Mayor and Aldermen of the said Cities for the time being, shall respectively at all times, have the power to regulate, restrict, and control the acts and doings of said Corporation, which may affect the health, safety, and convenience of the inhabitants of the said Cities respectively.

SECT. 4. No shares in the capital stock of said Corporation shall be issued for a less sum or amount, to be actually paid in on each, than the par value of the shares which shall be first issued. (Approved by the Governor, April 15, 1850).

In 1854 a charter was granted to Benjamin L. Allen, William A. Hayes, James C. Dunn, their associates and successors, incorporating them as the Shawmut Gas Light Company.

The Act is as follows :

Be it enacted by the Senate and House of Representatives, in General Court assembled, and by the authority of the same, as follows :

SECT. 1. Benjamin L. Allen, William A. Hayes, James C. Dunn, their associates and successors, are hereby made a Corporation, by the name of the Shawmut Gas Light Company, in the City of Boston, for the purpose of manufacturing and selling gas in the City of Boston; with all the powers and privileges, and subject to all the duties, restrictions, and liabilities, set forth in the thirty-eighth and forty-fourth chapters of the Revised Statutes.

SECT. 2. Said Corporation may hold real and personal estate, necessary and convenient for the said purpose, in amount not exceeding five hundred thousand dollars.

SECT. 3. Said Corporation, with the consent of the Mayor and Aldermen of the City of Boston, shall have power and authority to open the ground in any part of the streets, lanes, and highways, in said City, for the purpose of sinking and repairing such pipes and conductors as it may be necessary to sink for the purpose aforesaid; and the said Corporation after opening the ground in said streets, lanes, and highways, shall be held to put the same into repair, under the penalty of being prosecuted for a nuisance : *provided*, that the said Mayor and Aldermen for the time being, shall at all times have the power to regulate, restrict, and control all the acts and doings of said Corporation, which may in any manner affect the health, safety, and convenience of the inhabitants of said City.

SECT. 4. No shares in the capital stock of said Company shall be issued for a less sum or amount, to be actually paid in on each, than the par value of the shares which shall be first issued.

SECT. 5. This Act shall take effect from and after its passsage. (Approved by the Governor, April 15, 1854).

The same year the Suffolk Gas Company,—George Odiorne, who, as appears from the records hereafter cited, claimed to act for the Corporation, being a member of the Board of Aldermen,—applied for leave to open the streets to lay pipes.

The Shawmut Gas Light Company, one of these Corporations,—B. L. Allen being also a member of the Board of Aldermen,—also applied for leave to open the streets. Neither of these petitions are now to be found on the files of the Board of Aldermen. These petitions were referred to the Committee on Paving, which Committee made a Report, a copy of which is as follows:

SUFFOLK AND SHAWMUT GAS LIGHT COMPANIES.

CITY OF BOSTON.

In Board of Mayor and Aldermen,
Monday July 18th, 1854.

The Committee on Paving, to which was referred the petitions of the Suffolk and Shawmut Gas Companies, for leave to lay down pipes in our streets, and the remonstrance of the Boston Gas Light Company against the same, have considered the subject, and

REPORT:

The Boston Gas Light Company have had the exclusive privilege of furnishing gas to the citizens of Boston for several years, and their works are now in such a state of perfection that they need fear but little from the competition of other and new companies. The advantages of their long and varied experience; the favorable location of their works; the enhanced value of their real estate, owing to the many public and private improvements initiated and completed by our enterprising citizens, give them an almost overpowering superiority in any contest for business with a new company. No valid objection can be interposed by them, on the score of "vested rights," as the City has settled that principle, after a protracted and earnest contest with the Boston Aqueduct Corporation. In view then of the rapid growth of our City, and the contemplated and certain annexation of surrounding cities and towns at no distant date, we think the time has come for another Gas Company to be established in our midst. Other cities have a plurality of Gas Companies, and we are satisfied that business enough for two of them will be found in our City, and they can work together in generous and harmonious rivalry. The only important objection that need be mentioned, is an apprehension lest our streets and underground City works, during the progress of laying and repairing the pipes of the new Company, might be seriously disturbed. This is an important consideration, but should not be one, in our judgment, to override the good that will result to the citizens by the establishment of another company. It is also sufficient reply to this objection, that the work of taking up the pavement, &c., will be done under the direction of the Superintendent of Streets, acting under the orders of the Committee on Paving, and that all the expense thereof, and the damages consequent thereto, will be borne by the Company. The Committee believe that the public good would be promoted by the establishment in this City of another Gas Company, and they have the presumption to suppose that they and their successors can arrange this matter so as to place no material obstruction to the travel and trade of the City, and no injury to its streets or underground works. In view of the foregoing considerations, they recommend the passage of the following Order.

For the Committee,

GEORGE F. WILLIAMS, *Chairman.*

Ordered, That whenever it shall appear to the satisfaction of the Mayor for the time being, that the Suffolk and Shawmut Gas Companies are consolidated, and fifty per cent. of the Capital Stock actually paid in cash, permission shall be granted to said consolidated Company to open the streets for the purpose of laying their pipes, the work to be done under the direction of the Committee on Paving and Superintendent of Streets.

On motion of Alderman Allen, one of the corporators, this order was adopted.

It will be seen hereafter from the records of these Companies, that neither of them had, up to this time, held a meeting or accepted its Act of incorporation, or taken any steps towards an organization.

In 1855, the Legislature passed an Act, a copy of which is as follows :

Be it enacted by the Senate and House of Representatives, in General Court assembled, and by the authority of the same, as follows :

SECT. 1. The Shawmut Gas Light Company, and the Suffolk Gas Company are hereby authorized at meetings called for that purpose, and by votes to which a majority in number and value of the proprietors in each Company shall assent, to unite themselves as one Company, under the name of the Shawmut Gas Light Company ; and when such votes shall have been passed, they shall thereupon become one Company, with the name aforesaid ; and all the franchises, property, power, and privileges that may then be enjoyed by either ; and all the restrictions, liabilities, and obligations that may then belong to either, shall appertain to such united Company, in the same manner as if the same had been contained in or required by an original charter : *provided,* that if in opening any streets or ways, or in sinking or repairing any pipes or other fixtures, the said Company shall break or injure any mains, service pipes, or fixtures belonging to the Boston Gas Light Company, the said Shawmut Gas Light Company shall be responsible for all damage caused thereby.

SECT. 2. This Act shall take effect from and after its passage. (Approved by the Governor, May 15, 1855.)

It will appear hereafter that the Shawmut Gas Light Company held its first meeting, to accept its original charter, June 11, 1855.

An organization of the Suffolk Gas Light Company was attempted to be made March 21, 1856, which as the records themselves show, was entirely illegal and void.

It will also appear that the two Companies accepted the Act of May 15, 1855, uniting the two Corporations, and adopted a code of By-Laws, and elected as Directors, B. L. Allen, J. C. Dunn, and George Odiorne, and fixed the capital stock of the Shawmut Gas Light Company at $12,000, divided into 120 shares of $100 each. These By-Laws were adopted, and officers elected at a meeting held April 12, 1856.

It will also appear that no other meeting of the Corporation took place till January 4, 1860, although the last meeting was adjourned to 1857.

In February 29, 1860, an application was made to the Commissioners of Public Lands for the lease of some of the lands of the City at the South End.

The petition is given below with the proceedings of the Commissioners.

The fact that this petition had been made came to the knowledge of the undersigned and others, and immediately the remonstrance now before your Board was prepared, the remonstrants not being at the time aware that the order of July 18, 1854, passed by the Board of Aldermen, existed.

Upon the petition of the Shawmut Gas Light Company before the Land Commissioners a hearing was had, and the following proceedings took place. ·

At a Meeting of the Board of Land Commissioners, held February 29th, 1860, the following communication was received:—

Boston, February 29th, 1860.

To the Honorable Board of Land Commissioners.

GENTLEMEN,—We have entered into a conditional agreement to construct Gas Works for the Shawmut Gas Light Company, for the purpose of furnishing an abundant supply of gas in Boston, more particularly for the southern section of the City. We wish to contract with the City for a lease of the wharf owned by them, situated on the South Bay Lands, near the foot of Malden street, and adjoining wharf leased to G. R. Campbell & Co. This lot, according to the plans we have examined, is 220 feet on Albany street, 180 feet deep from Albany street to the Commissioners' line, containing 33,000 feet of solid wharf, and 20,800 feet of pile wharf. We wish to lease this lot for ten years, on the terms on which you have leased the other wharf, which is, we believe, one thousand dollars per annum, without taxes, with the right to purchase the land at the expiration of this term, at such price as you may now fix, payable by yearly instalments, or in such other way as may seem preferable.

We propose to commence the erection of our works immediately, and shall be ready to supply gas in the early fall ; and the agreement will be conditioned on our commencing the works at once, and finishing them with all reasonable dispatch.

Will you please fix the lowest price on these lands, that you deem proper, as this is an undertaking in which the whole City have a great interest; we know our request will be received in a liberal spirit.

An immediate decision is necessary, as we have no time to lose, all our plans depending upon our location.

We are yours, respectfully,

(Signed,)   GARDINER G. HUBBARD,
                   JOSEPH H. CONVERSE.

Voted, To refer the petition to a committee, consisting of Messrs. Preston, Howard, and Robbins.

At a meeting of the Board, held March 15th, the Committee, to whom was referred the petition of the Shawmut Gas Company, submitted a verbal report to the effect that they had given the parties a hearing, but preferred that the Board should take such action as they might deem expedient; when, upon motion, it was

Voted, That, in the opinion of this Board, it is expedient to lease, for a term of ten years, Wharf No. 3, South Bay.

Voted, That when this Board adjourn, it shall be to Saturday, the 17th inst., at 4, P. M.

Voted, That the Superintendent notify Messrs. Hubbard and Converse, of the Shawmut Gas Company, to meet this Board on Saturday, at 4, P. M.

The vote deeming it expedient to lease Wharf No. 3, South Bay, to the Shawmut Gas Company, for a term of ten years, was not approved by the Mayor.

At a meeting of the Board, held Saturday, March 17th, Mr. Converse was present for the purpose of giving such information respecting the intentions of the Company relative to the erection of buildings for the manufacturing of gas, should they lease said wharf; also such other information as the Board might require;—after retiring, the following vote was passed :—

Voted, "That the vote passed by this Board at its last meeting, whereby it was deemed expedient to lease Wharf No. 3, South Bay, to the Shawmut Gas Company for a period of 10 years," be rescinded.

Voted, That the petitioners have leave to withdraw.

2

At a meeting of the Board, held March 22d, the following communication was received :—

To the Honorable Board of Land Commissioners.

GENTLEMEN,—We are informed that some fears have been expressed, lest the erection of Gas Works, as proposed by the Shawmut Gas Light Company, would be an injury to adjacent lands in the City. From our experience in these matters, we believe that Gas Works can be constructed, with all the modern improvements, so as to remove every supposed objection of this nature.

The hearing before the Board on Saturday last, was, in the absence of one of the undersigned from the City, and also in the absence of the Engineer of the Company, John H. Blake, Esq.; wherefore they pray your honorable Board to grant them an opportunity of presenting their views upon the above points, and also upon the wishes of residents of Ward 11, for a better supply of gas than they now have.

(Signed,)   GARDINER G. HUBBARD,
JOSEPH H. CONVERSE.

Boston, March 21st, 1860.

Voted, That the petitioners be heard at the next regular meeting of this Board, and that they be notified by the Secretary.

At a meeting of the Board of Land Commissioners, held April 6th, 1860, Messrs. Blake, Emery, and Converse, presented themselves and were heard in behalf of the Shawmut Gas Company, relative to the objections raised against their locating any buildings for the manufacturing of gas upon any land belonging to the City of Boston. After retiring, upon motion being made, it was

Voted, That this Board adhere to its former action, passed March 17th, 1860.

Attest :   R. W. HALL,
Sup't Public Lands.

While the proceedings were pending, the remonstrance, a copy of which is given hereafter, was circulated, and on March 19, 1860, one of the remonstrances was presented to your Board.

On the same day, an order was offered by Alderman Pierce, as follows :—

CITY OF BOSTON.

In Board of Aldermen, March 19th, 1860.

Whereas, in the month of August, 1854, the following Order was passed :—

Ordered, That whenever it shall appear to the satisfaction of the Mayor for the time being, that the Suffolk and Shawmut Gas Companies are consolidated, and fifty per cent. of the capital stock actually paid in cash, permission shall be granted to the said consolidated Company to open the streets for the purpose of laying their pipes, the work to be done under the direction of the Committee on Paving and Superintendent of Streets.

And it having been publicly announced that sundry persons are the holders of the said charters, and propose to establish Gas Works and lay pipes in this City,—

It is ordered that this subject be referred to the Committee on Paving, to ascertain whether said Companies can now avail themselves of this permission, without further action of this Board, and to report whether it is expedient to modify or rescind said order.

Passed.

SAM'L F. McCLEARY, *City Clerk.*

At the same time the remonstrance was referred to the Committee on Paving.

The Committee on Paving held a meeting upon the subject of the order of inquiry, April 7th, 1860, at which the remonstrants were notified to be present. The Shawmut Gas Light Company were also present, and offered to the Committee an opinion of Sidney Bartlett, Esq., which is as follows :—

I have examined the several statutes incorporating the Suffolk Gas Company, and the Shawmut Gas Light Company, and the act of May 15, 1855, authorizing their union and conferring on the Corporations, when united, the powers, privileges and duties, that previously belonged to either of them, and the vote or order of the Mayor and Aldermen, passed 28th August, 1854, and am of opinion that, upon compliance with the conditions of that order, said united Company are, by virtue of the acts of the Legislature, authorized to open and use the streets of Boston for the purposes and in the manner set forth in the acts, and that said order cannot be legally revoked by the Mayor and Aldermen, even if said Corporation had not proceeded subsequently to make expenditures and alter its condition in faith of such order.

The power of the Legislature to authorize the use of highways for purposes not inconsistent with the uses for which they are laid out, is at least, so far as towns and cities are concerned, (and even without their consent,) I suppose not now controverted; and if this were doubtful, the assent of such towns or cities removes the doubt.

The right rests upon legislative grant; without its authority the City would be powerless in the matter. If, therefore, the grant has been once made effectual by the formal assent of the City authorities, which the grant requires as a condition, it has then become absolute, and the Mayor and Aldermen cannot repeal a legislative grant by a subsequent revocation of such assent.

The next question is, whether the assent of the Mayor and Aldermen is any the more revocable, because it was made dependent upon the consolidation of the two Corporations, and the payment in of capital; and, in my judgment, after a successful application to the Legislature to enable the parties to perform one part of the condition, and after all the conditions have been fairly performed, the assent of the Mayor and Aldermen became absolutely unqualified, and incapable of being revoked. Indeed the City would, upon familiar principles, be forever legally stopped from such revocation, upon the obvious ground that upon faith of their action the new Corporation had not only obtained a legislative grant, but made very considerable expenditures in the prosecution of the work.

(Signed,)   S. BARTLETT.

Boston, April 6th, 1860.

The hearing was adjourned to give the Shawmut Gas Light Company an opportunity to prove the facts on which the opinion of Mr. Bartlett was based, and for other evidence of the parties. At the adjournment, the opinion of Hon. B. R. Curtis was presented by the remonstrants to the Committee,—it was as follows:

CASE.

In 1850, the Suffolk Gas Company was incorporated by the Legislature of Massachusetts. The third section of their charter was as follows:

"Said Corporation shall have power and authority to open the ground in any part of the streets, lanes, and highways, in either of said Cities, with the consent of the Mayor and Aldermen thereof, for the purpose of sinking and repairing such pipes and conductors as it may be necessary to sink for the purpose aforesaid; and the said Corporation, after opening the ground in said streets, lanes, and highways, shall be held to put the same in repair, under the penalty of being prosecuted for a nuisance ; *provided*, that the Mayor and Aldermen of the said Cities for the time being, shall respectively at all times have the power to regulate, restrict, and control the acts and doings of said Corporation, which may in any manner affect the health, safety, and convenience of the inhabitants of the said Cities respectively."

In 1854, the Shawmut Gas Company was incorporated under a charter precisely similar to the first, except that it was limited to Boston.

In July, 1854, upon the petition of these two Companies, the Mayor and Aldermen of the City of Boston passed the following Order : *

" *Ordered*, That whenever it shall appear to the satisfaction of the Mayor for the time being, that the Suffolk and Shawmut Gas Companies are consolidated, and fifty per cent. of the capital stock actually paid in cash, permission shall be granted to said consolidated Company to open the streets for the purpose of laying their pipes, the work to be done under the direction of the Committee on Paving and the Superintendent of Streets."

In 1855, the Legislature passed an Act to enable these two Companies to unite into one Corporation, and granting such new Corporation all the franchises, property, powers, and privileges, enjoyed by either Company at the time of the union.

The two Companies being united, the questions arise, whether by force of the aforesaid Order of the Mayor and Aldermen, the new Company now has the consent of the Mayor and Aldermen of the City of Boston to open the streets of the City ? and if so, whether such consent is revocable ?

OPINION.

The vote of the Mayor and Aldermen is capable of being interpreted either as an assurance that at some future time, and upon compliance with certain conditions, consent would be given, or as a present grant of the assent of the Board, upon conditions to be complied with before acting thereon. The language of the Order points strongly to the former construction. It does not say permission is hereby granted, to be used when conditions shall be complied with ; but when certain things shall have been done, *permission shall be granted.*

* The Order was *passed* Aug. 28 ; the Committee on Paving *recommended* the passage of it July 18, and it is printed in the City Documents under that date ; No. 61.

It would seem, also, that a right or privilege conferred by such a prospective vote, upon condition that two corporations shall be consolidated into a third, cannot be deemed a privilege vested in either of these Corporations at the time of their union, because the consent to open the streets was not granted to either of them.

The vote was in effect a declaration made to these two Corporations, that if the Legislature should enable them to unite into a third Company, permission to open the streets would then be granted to such new Company.

I entertain, also, considerable doubt whether an unlimited term of years was intended to be allowed for compliance with the prescribed conditions; and whether, by fair intendment, it should not be understood that the conditions must be complied with, and the privilege exercised, within a reasonable time after the passage of the Order; and if so, I should hardly think five years after the passage of the Act of Consolidation would be deemed such reasonable time.

But however this may be, I am of opinion that by the true construction of the third section of the charter, this Corporation can open no street of the City, for the purpose of sinking their pipes, without the consent of the Mayor and Aldermen actually existing and operative at the time of doing the act; and that any consent, however formally given, may be revoked or modified at any time before the streets are opened, if the Board for the time being shall deem it proper to do so in reference to the health, safety, and convenience of the inhabitants.

This charter is to be fairly examined and reasonably and justly expounded, and is not to receive a strained interpretation adverse to the Corporation; but when thus examined, if there be a fair doubt whether a privilege which may be burdensome or injurious to the public has been granted, that doubt must be solved in favor of the public and against the Corporation. And especially must this rule of interpretation be kept in view when construing reservations of power made by the Legislature in behalf of the public, to protect from injury the health, safety, and convenience of the inhabitants of a great City.

Now, this third section of the charter first grants to the Corporations the privilege of opening the ground in any part of the streets, with the consent of the Mayor and Aldermen. If it had stopped here, I think it would be difficult to maintain that such consent, when once given, could never be recalled, and that the Corporation could begin to execute the license five years after it was given, and in opposition to the will of the Mayor and Aldermen for the time being, who should adjudge the execution injurious to the public.

Considering the nature of the act to be done, and the purpose of the Legislature in requiring the assent of the Mayor and Aldermen, it would seem that such consent must exist when the act is done, and be founded on the then state of things; and not that at some indefinite preceding time, and founded on then existing facts, some other Board had consented.

But however this might be, if this part of the section stood alone, the proviso which follows the grant of power, and is manifestly intended to qualify it, leaves no doubt in my mind that the Mayor and Aldermen may interfere at any time, and prohibit the Corporation from opening the ground of these streets, if in their judgment the health, safety, and convenience of the citizens would be in any manner affected by such opening.

The language of the proviso is very broad, and capable of being understood as going much further than this. But whatever else it may apply to, I can entertain no doubt that it was designed to perform the usual and strictly appropriate office of a proviso; which is to qualify, or explain, or restrict, the enactment to which it is attached, and that its effect is to enact in clear terms that no consent of one Board shall deprive the Mayor and Aldermen for the time being of power to restrain the Corporation from opening the ground in any part of the streets, lanes, or highways of the City.

And I am of opinion that if the Mayor and Aldermen should pass an Order repealing the Order of 1854, and declaring that the Shawmut Gas Company shall not open the ground in any street of the City, that Corporation would have no legal right or power to do so.

(Signed,)   B. R. CURTIS.

The Committee also had procured an opinion of the City Solicitor, which is as follows:

I think it is competent for the two Companies named, when they have been consolidated, and fifty per cent. of their capital has been paid in, to open the streets for laying pipes, &c.—if this Order remains unrescinded; and I am also of the opinion that the Board of Aldermen may rescind the Order, if they see fit to do so, and that upon the rescision thereof the right will no longer exist.

(Signed,)   J. P. HEALY.

March 22, 1860.

The remonstrants then offered evidence on the subject referred to in the remonstrances. They first offered the remonstrances themselves, which are as follows:

To the Honorable, the Mayor and Aldermen of the City of Boston:

Represent the undersigned owners or occupants of real estate in the Southern Wards of the City, that they have been informed, through the public prints, that a new Gas Company is about to be organized; and they have heard, from other sources, that such Company is now negotiating with the City of Boston for the purchase of some of the City Lands on South Bay, or Back Bay, so called, for the location of their Works, and intend to make application to your Board for leave to erect such Works, and to open the streets for the purpose of laying their pipes.

They, therefore, most earnestly remonstrate against any sale, by the City of Boston, of any portion of the City Lands for the purpose aforesaid, and against granting leave to any Company to erect Works for the manufacture of Gas, in the Southern part of the City, or to open the streets for the purpose of laying down pipes.

And they show as reasons therefor:

That it is now the established policy of this City to encourage the erection of first-class dwelling houses at the South End, and especially upon the lands which have recently been purchased from the City.

That large amounts of money have been expended by the City, in laying out broad and elevated streets, and extensive Parks, or Squares, with that end in view.

That all the sales of the City Lands, for many years past, have been made with restrictions and conditions against the erection of any other buildings than dwelling houses or stores.

That the undersigned, and many others, have bought such lands, subject to such conditions, or the houses built thereon, or have leased the same, relying, as they had a right to do, upon the solemn pledge which a policy of the City has given, to wit: that nothing should be done by the City, or permitted, if within its power to prevent, which should tend to impair the value of their property, or render their dwellings less comfortable or agreeable.

That the erection of Works for the manufacture of Gas, in any part of the South End, would create a nuisance so intolerable as greatly to injure and depreciate the value of all real estate in that section of the City, as well the property of individual citizens as of the City, a large amount of whose lands are yet unsold, and so would be a very great public, as well as private calamity.

That the present condition of the Northern portion of the City, in the vicinity of the Works of the Boston Gas Light Company, now nearly or quite abandoned as a place of genteel residence, and given over, in a great part, to a foreign population, clearly and forcibly demonstrates the impolicy of permitting the erection of Gas Works near the more thickly settled portions of the City, and compels them to remonstrate the more earnestly against the erection of Gas Works in their own immediate neighborhood.

That the laying of the pipes of a new Company, in the streets already occupied by sewers, water pipes and gas pipes beneath the surface, and in some streets, by railroad tracks upon the surface, and the necessity of taking up the streets hereafter, for the relaying or repair of said pipes, is of itself a sufficient reason why no new Company should be permitted to open the streets, unless some great exigency requires such course; therefore, they earnestly remonstrate against the sale, by the City, of lands for the purpose mentioned, and against any permission to erect Gas Works at the South End, and against granting leave to open the streets to lay pipes therein.

And they pray that, in case of any movement contemplating the erection of said Works, over which the City authorities have any control whatever, they may be heard before your honorable Board in opposition thereto.

Alvin Adams,
Charles G. Greene,
Josiah M. Jones,
Aaron Kimball,
Pliny Nickerson,
William Shutz,
George R. Carter,
James A. Pierce,
R. D. Goodwin,
George L. Goodwin,
F. W. Choate,
John C. Morse,
Jonas H. French,
A. B. Butterfield,
Nathaniel Winsor,
Mason Morse,
Sylvester Bowman,
Oliver Ditson,
George B. Cartwright,
S. H. Barnes,
A. Tompkins,
John T. Wells,
Noble H. Hill,
W. H. Baldwin,

William W. Clapp, Jr.,
Charles Torrey,
Charles S. Kendall,
Carlos W. Pierce,
J. Lockwood,
C. F. Knight,
Charles K. Cobb,
George Pierce,
Thomas T. Litchfield,
William Lumb,
George E. Betton,
Francis Boyd,
E. T. Milliken,
William T. Hart,
R. S. Wade,
Andrew G. Briggs,
William Babson,
C. Curry,
C. E. Fuller,
C. B. Wood,
Charles A. Babcock,
Harvey Jewell,
F. W. Sawyer,
John C. Pratt,

3

Charles Emerson,
Alden Speare,
J. C. Dana,
A. G. Farwell,
Stephen Tilton,
Tilton, Wheelwright & Co.,
Amos B. Merrill,
S. H. Lewis,
A. W. Ladd,
Geo. P. Denney,
Joseph H. Gray,
Nathaniel Cleaves,
C. H. Carruth,
H. Farnum Smith,
William K. Bacall,
J. O. Shapleigh,
Charles Carruth,
W. Whittemore,
E. Gerry Dudley,
R. Warner,
Henry H. Hyde,
B. F. Horn,
John G. Wetherbee,
Bradford Durfee,
Austin Levanseller,
Stephen Fitzgerald,
Charles Allen,
M. J. Chapin,
Edward A. Morse,
J. F. Came,
A. F. Chandler,
L. G. Parmelee,
Charles B. Hall,
A. N. Cook,
Henry L. Hallett,
M. W. Cobb,
Thomas Cobb,
A. R. Wentworth,
Walter Herbert Judson,
Frank A. Field,
F. W. Sawyer,
Thomas C. Porter,

Levi C. Barney,
Russell W. Burke,
J. B. Tilton,
James C. Bayley,
Henry W. Warren,
L. A. Cutler,
J. B. Bartlett,
Moses W. Richardson,
William H. Harding,
James D. Kent,
S. G. Taylor,
J. W. Hobbs,
John Gove,
John H. Shapleigh,
Charles E. Thayer,
Jane Sweetser,
George H. Burke,
T. Willey,
Paul D. Wallis,
G. B. DuBois,
J. K. Porter,
N. C. Poor,
Sawyer S. Stone,
C. B. Wilson,
J. W. Tower,
A. F. Wilkinson,
M. J. Morse,
Charles C. Henshaw,
Ephraim Allen,
Thomas H. Fuller,
Samuel D. Crane,
J. D. Roberts,
William Lang,
George A. Bramer,
Tyler Batcheller,
C. M. Jordan,
Edward Punne,
William C. Dunham,
George W. Kendall,
Albert Mortimer,
Jonas H. French,
William Beals, Jr.,

Philip A. Locke,
H. S. Chase,
H. Gilbert,
C. W. Galloupe,
George P. Marston,
David Chapin,
N. D. Silsbee,
C. Gilbert,
J. A. Bamford,
H. H. Curtis,
R. A. Upton,
F. P. Sanger,
S. M. Lawrence,
J. B. Dudley,
M. M. Fales,
E. Blodget,
William G. Tyler,
Samuel H. Smith,
Addison Swallow,
Charles H. Gilman,
Francis Howard,
Wilson Comer,
James Stewart,
S. B. Conant,
A. H. Horn.
G. D. Gale,
E. W. Marden,
W. E. Peaver,
Moses M. Allen,
Wm. B. Fowle, Jr.,
J. A. Page,
James M. Wheeler,
C. Norris,
Geo. S. Harris,
Leopold Herman,
Augustus Lothrop,
H. W. Suter,
John P. Bigelow,
John Wade,
James B. Berry,
James M. Vose,
S. P. Tolman,

A. A. Ranney,
William C. King,
W. T. Haskell,
Edward Cabot,
G. T. Cleary,
J. Trull,
Francis Allen,
A. Nason,
Thomas H. Dyer,
George K. Townsend,
A. Pearsans,
William R. Chaffee,
E. T. Follansbee,
J. A. Carr,
Alex. Ferguson,
David Corbett,
T. S. Gale,
E. G. Morrison,
F. P. Conant,
Henry Schroeder,
E. S. Johnson,
Edward Lang,
L. S. M'Intire,
J. G. Hall,
W. B. Wadman,
Hiram Johnson,
G. H. Maynard,
W. M. Maynard,
Robert Orr,
George D. Wise,
S. C. Shapleigh,
Wm. P. Tenny,
Edw. W. Dean,
Charles Rollins,
William H. Smith,
Thomas J. Whidden,
G. F. Thayer,
F. F. Dewey,
Jas. M. Torrey,
Edw. T. Russell, Jr.,
C. F. Crehore,
Hugh Earl,

John F. Pierce,
Alex. Fullerton,
David Hunt,
C. C. Gore,
Charles H. Appleton,
James A. Dix,
Joseph Carew,
M. M'Cormick,
E. F. Robinson,
William Collier,
John Coulehan,
Robert Morse,
Thomas Rodgers,
Henry B. Stratton,
L. Munsell,
Martin Beatty,
H. W. Cushing,
Geo. C. Richardson,
Patrick O. Connor,
John Houatt,
Geo. W. Hunnewell,
John H. Shapleigh,
E. H. Sylvester,
Volney Wilder,
Seth Robinson,
J. P. Snow,
Oliver S. Osgood,
John C. Giles,
B. S. Shumway,
Geo. M. Guild,
L. W. Smalley,
J. A. Littlefield,
John Cassell,
Stephen Prince,
Stephen Wooden,
H. P. Hickey,
A. Clark,
W. R. Clapp,
B. W. Gilbert,
G. D. Whitmore,
John Carleton,
F. Ingersoll,

Henry N. Clark,
Luther Parks, Jr.,
Edward S. Babbitt,
F. H. Williams,
Francis R. Josselyn,
Henry A. Wainwright,
Alfred A. Mudge,
R. M. Merson,
Wm. C. Poland,
John Forrest,
William W. Collier,
Alfred R. Glover,
George W. Josselyn,
Geo. S. Robertson,
E. P. Winslow,
Chas. H. Mills,
Robert Gow,
David H. Jacobs,
Geo. Solomons,
John Shea,
Joseph Coffey,
Louis D. Whittemore,
Charles H. Call,
H. C. Pinkham,
Malcolm Donety,
Geo. P. Upham,
Thomas W. Robinson,
Albert Carter,
Henry White,
G. R. Campbell,
Amasa Harmon,
Thomas F. Hinckley,
W. L. Weeks,
T. Stratton,
M. O. Shattuck,
Isord B. Lewis,
Wm. P. Tower,
S. N. Gould,
E. Osgood,
W. J. Mercer,
Wm. Parkman, Jr.,
B. R. Gilbert,

M. H. Learnard,
H. F. Marsh,
R. P. Haines,
Wm. Parkman,
Wm. T. Hart,
William Rice,
A. Jacobs,
N. Crowell, Jr.,
William H. Bird,
John Sharland,
Henry Brown,
I. W. Domett,
Wm. H. Baker,
Albert H. Rhodes,
Sol. Sweetser,
Jas. D. Martin,
J. S. Rutledge,
W. H. Learned, Jr.,
Henry Dawes,
J. Meyer,
S. H. Leonard,
F. Henry Dix,
John Jeffries, Jr.,
Henry Fowle,
Geo. H. Peters,
Jno. Gouldsbury,
Wm. Leggate,
Charles H. Allen,
J. Bardwell,
Edwin B. Houghton,
James M. Wheeler,
C. J. Bishop,
James Hartshorn, Jr.,
B. F. Campbell, Jr.,
L. M. Clark,
H. D. P. Bigelow,
Dan'l Harwood,
Gilbert Nash,
Chas. H. Rhodes,
Geo. F. Emery,
N. Broughton,
Wm. Capen,

P. Stephenson,
G. A. P. Darling,
C. W. Cottrell,
Thomas B. Hawkes,
S. P. Bennett,
David Pulsifer,
Charles H. Blanchard,
D. D. Dickinson,
G. W. Hunkins,
J. R. Marshall,
R. A. Robertson,
Wm. Bird,
George Darling,
E. F. Leland,
J. A. Lane,
Thomas Kidder,
Wm. Jones,
J. J. McNutt,
Lewis Currier,
Francis T. Church,
John M. Bradbury,
S. A. Dix,
Geo. A. Doane,
Sam'l A. Way,
John Wetherbee, Jr.,
George G. Gove,
Wm. C. Merriam,
J..B. Brown,
H. S. Cushing,
A. H. Sylvester,
Chas. H. Hunt,
J. W. Bradley,
Jno. K. Grout,
A. H. Kimball,
Wm. L. Eliot,
A. P. Nash,
T. W. Beamis,
Stimson Leach,
W. R. Broughton,
W. H. Curtis,
Wm. Orne,
George Cullis,

E. P. Cassell,
Watson Gore, Jr.,
J. Edward Dodd,
E. E. Plimpton,
Chas. B. F. Adams,
Samuel Bradley,
M. W. Richardson,
C. H. Chandler,
B. F. Rollins,
Robert H. Clouston, Jr.,
S. B. Hopkins,
N. C. Wayne,
Henry W. B. Frost,
A. Storrs,
E. L. Prestman,
William Noble,
H. M. Currier,
Henry A. Gane,
E. W. Arnold, Jr.,
Geo. Cushing,

Samuel Curtis,
John G. Broughton,
E. D. Cassell,
Silas Allen,
Benjamin Thaxter,
Nathan'l Bradlee,
Gardner Murphy,
Enoch Bride,
A. G. Conant,
H. D. Williams,
Sam'l McMinch,
S. B. Krogman,
Levi Philbrook,
John H. Bazin,
W. C. Montgomery,
Chas. H. Noyes,
Joseph H. Gray,
Edwin R. Sawyer,
Benjamin Lyon,
Isaac Sweetser.

The oral evidence of the remonstrants and proceedings, as reported in the Boston Transcript, are as follows:

THE NEW GAS WORKS AT THE SOUTH END. An adjourned hearing was held at 12 o'clock to-day, before the Committee on Paving, to consider the subject of rescinding a former order of the Board of Aldermen, giving leave to the Shawmut Gas Company to put down pipes in certain streets at the South part of the City. Alderman Willis, Chairman of the Committee, and Aldermen Holbrook and Faxon, were present.

Oliver Stevens and G. G. Hubbard, Esqrs., appeared for the consolidated Shawmut and Suffolk Gas Companies; and Harvey Jewell and John S. Holmes, Esqrs., for the remonstrants.

The Chairman stated that the City Solicitor had given an official opinion that the present Board of Aldermen had power to revoke the order in question, when considerable discussion ensued as to which side should put in their case first.

Mr. Jewell reminded the Committee that, at the last meeting, it was understood that the parties in interest should to-day show whether the two Companies, the Suffolk and Shawmut, had been legally consolidated and organized, and whether they had made any considerable expenditure of money, entitling them to the protection of the City Government.

He then read an opinion of Ex-Judge B. R. Curtis, against the power of the new Company to proceed under the original order passed in 1855 ; if they had any power it should have been exercised within a reasonable time, certainly less than five years after the granting of the charter; and that the Board of Aldermen had complete authority to rescind the order, for the benefit of the health or other interests of the citizens.

Mr. Stevens said the Companies could not be made to appear here as petitioners. They held the right to open the streets, by authority of the Board in 1855, and having consolidated agreeably to Act of the Legislature, they stood under the action of the City Government, and were in fact remonstrants against any interference with their rights.

Mr. Holmes said the Companies stood as petitioners, and had caused this hearing.

Mr. Stevens replied that they had never petitioned for any hearing, but simply asked to be notified if there was to be one.

The Chairman said the question was on rescinding the original order.

Mr. Jewell did not understand why the other side were so unwilling to show their hand, if they had so good a case as they claimed.

Alderman Holbrook took the ground that the remonstrants against the proposed action of the Companies should first present their case.

Alderman Faxon thought the Companies should proceed to show their rights, as it was understood at the last meeting that they were to do so.

The Chairman decided that the remonstrants should proceed first.

Mr. Holmes said they were quite willing to do this, as they had the opinions of the City Solicitor and Judge Curtis, also several remonstrances with hundreds of signatures.

Mr. Jewell presented three remonstrances, signed by W. W. Clapp, Jr., and numerous others, and then proceeded to call evidence.

Mr. W. W. Clapp, Jr., said it would be a perfect nuisance to open the streets at the South End for the purpose of laying the gas pipes. It would be a serious detriment to real estate, especially in and around West Chester Park.

In answer to a question, Mr. Clapp stated that the neighborhood referred to was amply supplied with gas. The people generally, of that section of the City, were against the formation of any new Gas Company. He further stated that he had no practical knowledge as regards the price of gas.

Mr. J. B. Richardson, a manufacturer of gas works, also a resident of the South End, remarked that at times there was not a sufficient supply of gas for the southern part of the City. He considered that the generating power for the production of gas, possessed by the Boston Gas Company, was amply sufficient, but in some portions of the ward in which he lived, the main was not large enough to supply the requisite amount of gas during some hours of the evening, between six and nine o'clock. This only applied to certain localities. Boston gas is better than New York—the price is the same as in Philadelphia and New York.

Mr. Richardson stated that gas could be made from coal, at its prices last season, and stored in the reservoir for distribution, for $1.25 per thousand cubic feet. The remaining expense would be the interest upon the capital employed, and the cost of conveying through the streets. He further remarked that as the population increased at the South End, the complaints in respect to the gas multiplied.

Mr. Francis Boyd saw no necessity for the organization of any new Gas Company or location in Ward Eleven. It would be perfectly impossible to locate a gas manufactory in Ward Eleven, without its being a great nuisance to the citizens during the summer season. After investigation, Mr. Boyd was satisfied with the quality of the gas produced by the Boston Gas Company; it was better than that of New York. The price of the gas of this City was low enough.

Mr. Francis Sawyer, who lived in Chester Park, observed that before the new company was talked about, he never heard any objections either to the quality, price or supply of gas, although there had been complaints about almost everything else. The people of that vicinity were universally opposed to another company. The opening of the streets would be a nuisance.

Mr. E. G. Dudley, a large real estate owner at the South End, gave it as his opinion that the supply of gas was ample. He had owned and had charge of fifty houses in Ward Eleven, and had never seen any reason to find fault as to the quantity of gas furnished by the present works.

Mr. S. Bowman, a resident at the corner of Chester and Washington streets, never had any trouble with the gas, although he lived in one of the largest houses in that quarter of the City. He thought there was only a slight difference in favor of Roxbury gas, for which $3.50 was charged. He did not see any advantage to the citizens of Boston, to arise from the competition of a new company.

Mr. Jewell read a note from Mr. G. F. Thayer, who resides in Ashland Place, strongly condemning the project of an additional company.

Mr. John T. Holmes, a resident of Milford street, and one of the counsel, said, that upon inquiry and study, he was satisfied that gas could not be manufactured cheaper than $2.25 per thousand cubic feet, and although he had once complained as loudly as anybody of the company, he was certain that his previous troubles arose from his management of the gas apparatus.

This closed the case in behalf of the remonstrants for the present.

The Chairman of the Committee said that it was incumbent upon the counsel for the new company to show that it had been properly organized, under the acts of the Legislature, and had fifty per cent. of its capital stock paid in.

Mr. Oliver Stevens said that this was not exactly the posture of the case. The Gas Company which he represented had been duly organized, and had negotiated for a site in Roxbury for their works.

It was not pretended that 50 per cent. of their capital had been paid, but it was being so rapidly accomplished, that parties had come in to remonstrate against their laying the pipes, as they would have the right to do, after this proportion of their capital stock had been received. The hearing was progressing when our report closed.

This closed the evidence of the remonstrants. The Shawmut Gas Light Company then put in their book of records, a true copy of which (the acts which have already been cited being omitted) is as follows :—

SHAWMUT GAS LIGHT COMPANY.

At a meeting of the grantees, named in the act of the Legislature of the Commonwealth of Massachusetts to incorporate the Shawmut Gas Light Company, held at the office of Wm. A. Hayes, No. 8 Merchants Bank Building, State street, Boston, pursuant to the following notice, published in the Boston Post, May 31st, 1855, and continued in every other publication of that paper until the meeting, also a copy of the notice sent to each of the parties named in the Charter,—

SHAWMUT GAS LIGHT COMPANY.

The first meeting of the grantees, named in the act to incorporate the Shawmut Gas Light Company and their Associates, will be held at No. 8 Merchants Bank Building, State street, Boston, on Monday, June 11th next, at 11 o'clock, in the forenoon, to accept if thought

4

proper the act of incorporation granted by the Legislature, and for the transaction of any other business that may come before them.

B. L. ALLEN, } Persons named
WM. A. HAYES, } in the act of
JAMES C. DUNN, } incorporation.

Boston, May 30th, 1855.

Present, Messrs. B. L. Allen, Jas. C. Dunn, Wm. A. Hayes. B. L. Allen, Esq., was chosen Chairman, and Wm. A. Hayes, Secretary. The notice calling the meeting was read by the Secretary. The following Act of Incorporation, granted to the Shawmut Gas Light Company, was read.

[Then follows the Act of 1854. Approved April 15, 1854.]

Voted, To accept the act of incorporation granted by the Legislature of the Commonwealth of Massachusetts to the Shawmut Gas Light Company.

Voted, That the members of this Corporation be, and are hereby declared to be, the following persons: Benj. L. Allen, Wm. A. Hayes, Jas. C. Dunn, and such others as shall hereafter become Stockholders, their associates, assigns, and legal representatives.

Voted, That of the present members of the Company, two shall constitute a quorum for the transaction of business, and that each member of the Company be notified of all meetings at least a day before a meeting.

Voted, To adjourn *sine die.*

Attest: WM. A. HAYES, *Secretary.*

Boston, June 11th, 1855.

At a meeting of the proprietors of the Shawmut Gas Light Company, held at No. 8 Merchants Bank Building, 28 State street, Boston, Friday, March 21st, 1856, pursuant to the following notice published in the Boston Post, March 14th, 1856, also on 17th, 19th, and 21st days of the same month, and also a written notice of the meeting and object of the meeting sent to each of the proprietors two days before the day of the meeting,—

NOTICE. — SHAWMUT GAS LIGHT COMPANY. A meeting of the proprietors of the Shawmut Gas Light Company will be held at

No. 8 Merchants Bank Building, 28 State street, Boston, on Friday, 21st inst., at 3½ o'clock, in the afternoon.

WILLIAM A. HAYES, *Secretary.*

Boston, March 13th, 1856.

Voted, That when this meeting adjourn, it be adjourned to meet in the same place, Saturday, 22d instant.

Voted, To adjourn.

Attest: WM. A. HAYES, *Secretary.*

At a meeting of the proprietors of the Shawmut Gas Light Company, held at No. 8 Merchants Bank Building, Saturday, March 22d, 1856, according to adjournment, B. L. Allen was re-chosen Chairman, and William A. Hayes, Secretary.

Voted, unanimously, That this Company accept the Charter granted by the Legislature to unite with the Suffolk Gas Company, and do hereby agree to unite with the same.

Voted, That this meeting be dissolved.

Attest: WM. A. HAYES, *Secretary.*

Boston, March 22d, 1856.

COPY OF THE RECORDS OF THE SUFFOLK GAS COMPANY.

Boston, March 21, 1856. At a meeting of the proprietors of the Suffolk Gas Company, holden at office No. 8 Merchants Bank Building, upon a call published in the Boston Daily Bee,—

NOTICE.

There will be a meeting of the proprietors of the Suffolk Gas Company, at the office No. 8 Merchants Bank Building, on Friday, the 21st inst., to act upon the question of the acceptance of the act of last year, to unite the Suffolk and Shawmut Gas Light Companies.

Per order of the proprietors,

GEO. ODIORNE.

Voted, To elect a Clerk *pro tempore,* and Geo. Odiorne, of Boston, was unanimously elected, and qualified.

Voted, To adjourn to Saturday, 22d inst., at 1¼ o'clock

(Signed,) GEORGE ODIORNE, *Clerk pro tem.*

COPY OF RECORDS OF SUFFOLK GAS COMPANY—*Continued.*

Boston, March 22*d,* 1856.

The proprietors of the Suffolk Gas Company met, according to adjournment.

Voted, To accept the act of the Legislature, passed incorporating the Suffolk Gas Company.

Voted, To accept the act of the Legislature, of May 15th, 1855, entitled "An Act to unite the Shawmut Gas Light Company and the Suffolk Gas Company."

Voted, That this Company, by the acceptance of the last named act, do agree to unite with the Shawmut Gas Light Company, according to the conditions of said act.

Voted, To adjourn to such time and place as the Clerk may deem it necessary to call another meeting.

Adjourned.

(Signed,)   GEO. ODIORNE, *Clerk pro tempore.*

At a meeting of the proprietors of the Shawmut Gas Light Company and the proprietors of the Suffolk Gas Company, held at No. 8 Merchants Bank Building, State street, Boston, Saturday, March 22d, 1856,—the meeting was called to order by B. L. Allen, Esq.

Voted, To proceed to the choice of a Secretary. Wm. A. Hayes was unanimously chosen.

Voted, To proceed to the choice of a Chairman. B. L. Allen, Esq. was unanimously chosen.

Voted, That the Shawmut Gas Light Company and the Suffolk Gas Company do unite, and are hereby united into one Company, under the name of the Shawmut Gas Light Company.

The above vote was passed unanimously.

The following copy of the act of incorporation, granted by the Legislature of the Commonwealth of Massachusetts, May, 1855, was read.

[Here follows a copy of the Act of 1855, to unite the Shawmut Gas Light Company and the Suffolk Gas Company. Approved May 15, 1855.]

Voted, unanimously, To accept the act of incorporation uniting the Shawmut Gas Light Company and the Suffolk Gas Company.

Voted, That the Secretary be authorized to prepare a Code of By-Laws, to be presented at the next meeting.

Voted, That when this meeting adjourn, it be adjourned to meet in the same place on Saturday next, the 29th inst.

Voted, To adjourn.

Attest: WM. A. HAYES, *Secretary.*

Boston, March 22, 1856.

At a meeting of the proprietors of the Shawmut Gas Light Company, held at No. 8 Merchants Bank Building, according to adjournment, Saturday, March 29th, 1856, a quorum not being present, it was

Voted, That the meeting be adjourned to meet in the same place, at such a time as the Secretary may deem it expedient to call a meeting.

Attest: WM. A. HAYES, *Secretary.*

Boston, March 29th, 1856.

At a meeting of the proprietors of the Shawmut Gas Light Company, held at No. 8 Merchants Bank Building, State street, Boston, Saturday, April 12th, 1856,—present, Messrs. B. L. Allen, J. C. Dunn, Geo. Odiorne, Wm. A. Hayes,—

The meeting was called to order by the Chairman, B. L. Allen, Esq.

The following Code of By-Laws was presented by the Secretary, and read.

BY-LAWS.

ARTICLE 1.   There shall be a stated meeting of the Stockholders of the Shawmut Gas Light Company on the third Wednesday of January, annually, at such time and place as the Directors shall determine.   At such stated meeting there shall be elected, by ballot, a Clerk, a Treasurer, and three Directors.   The Directors, and every other officer chosen by the Stockholders, shall hold their respective offices for the term of one year and until others shall be elected and qualified in their places, excepting that every Director shall cease to retain any office in the Company when he ceases to be a Stockholder; but the Directors and other officers chosen at this meeting shall hold their offices only until the annual meeting next to be holden according to this Article, and until others shall be chosen and qualified in their places.   Two of the Directors shall constitute a quorum for the transaction of business.   The Directors shall elect one of their number to be President of the Corporation, who shall preside at all their meetings and at all meetings of the Stockholders. In case of his absence, a President pro tempore shall be chosen by the Stockholders or by the Directors. The Directors may fill any vacancy which may happen in their Board, with the consent of two-thirds of the Directors remaining in office; and until such vacancy shall be supplied all the powers and authority conferred on the whole Board of Directors shall be held and enjoyed by such remaining Directors.

ART. 2. The annual meetings of the Stockholders shall be called by an advertisement, signed by the President or Clerk of the Corporation, and published in one or more newspapers at least seven days before the day appointed for the meeting. Special meetings of the Corporation shall be called in like manner whenever the Directors may deem it expedient, or whenever any three or more of the Stockholders representing at least one-quarter of the shares and interest, shall, in writing, require the President or Clerk to call such meeting.

ART. 3. At the meetings of the Corporation, all votes shall be given by the Stockholders in person or by proxy, and every Stockholder shall be entitled to as many votes as he holds shares. Authority to act as proxy, or to receive dividends, shall be in writing, signed by the proprietor, and the same, or a notarial copy thereof, shall be delivered to the Treasurer, and remain on his files.

ART. 4. At all meetings of the Stockholders three of the number who are entitled to vote and representing not less than one-third of the shares in interest, shall constitute a quorum, and whenever three such Stockholders shall not be present or represented at any such meeting the same shall be adjourned to such time and place as a majority of those present shall determine.

ART. 5. The Directors shall appoint such officers and agents as they deem necessary for the interest of the Corporation, who shall be removable at their pleasure. They shall also assign to them their respective duties and regulate their compensation and that of all the other officers of the Company. They may sell and cause to be transferred and conveyed any mortgages, promissory notes, and other securities or personal property of the Company, for such consideration and on such terms as they may think proper, and upon such sale may cause suitable and proper conveyances, valid in law, to be made thereof. They may cause such buildings, with or without machinery, to be erected as they may deem necessary or advantageous to the Company. They may purchase or sell such real estate or personal property as in their opinion will be for the interest of the Company. They shall declare all dividends, audit and approve all accounts, superintend the different officers and agents appointed by them, and exercise such other powers and authority as may be necessary or proper in the management of the affairs of the Corporation.

ART. 6. The Clerk, immediately after his election, shall be sworn to the faithful performance of his duties by a Justice of the Peace, and his oath shall be entered with the signature of the magistrate on the records of the Corporation. He shall attend all meetings of the Stockholders and of the Directors, and shall keep records of their doings in separate books. In his absence, a Clerk pro tempore shall be elected by the Stockholders or Directors who shall do all things whilst he remains in office required of the Clerk of the Corporation.

ART. 7. The Treasurer shall give bond with sureties to the satisfaction of the Directors for the faithful performance of his duties. He shall have an office in Boston accessible to all persons having business with the Corporation. He shall keep all deeds, promissory notes, and valuable papers of the Corporation; collect and receive all assessments, income, and moneys that may be due to the Corporation, and disburse the same as the Directors shall order. He shall sign and execute in behalf of the Corporation, all deeds, leases, or other obligations of the Corporation, when so instructed by the Stockholders or Directors. He shall keep a regular set of books containing the accounts of the Corporation and of its funds that pass through his hands. He shall make a complete settlement of the accounts and books annually, and as much oftener as the Board of Directors require. He shall render an account of his doings to the Stockholders at their annual meetings. He shall notify each Stockholder of all assessments at least ten days before the day fixed for the payment thereof. He shall issue certificates of stock to all persons entitled thereto, and keep suitable books showing the number of shares held by the respective Stockholders from time to time. In the absence of the Treasurer, a person shall be chosen by the Directors to fill the office pro tempore.

ART. 8. Every promissory note made in behalf of the Corporation shall be signed by the Treasurer, and shall be approved in writing on the face thereof by two or more of the Directors, and no others shall be sufficient and valid against the Corporation.

ART. 9. The Corporation shall have a Common Seal, to be preserved and kept by the Treasurer, and used by him, bearing the words and figures,—"Shawmut Gas Light Company, Incorporated May 15, 1855."

ART. 10. The capital stock of the Shawmut Gas Light Company is hereby fixed at $12,000, divided into 120 shares of $100 each. The holders of shares in the capital stock shall be entitled to certificates thereof, signed by the President, countersigned by the Treasurer, and authenticated by the Common Seal; and all certificates shall be in the following form, viz:

Shawmut Gas Light Company.

No.   Shares.

Be it known that   proprietor of   shares at $100 each, in the Capital Stock of the Shawmut Gas Light Company, subject to the provisions of the Charter and By-Laws of the Corporation.

Dated at Boston, this   day of   A. D. one thousand eight hundred

President.
Treasurer.

Form of Endorsement on Certificate of Stock:

Transfer No.

For value received,   hereby transfer to   of   shares of the Capital Stock of the Shawmut Gas Light Company, subject to the provisions of the Charter and By-Laws of the Corporation.

Witness my hand, this   day of   A. D. 18

ART. 11. The capital stock of the Shawmut Gas Light Company shall be paid at such times and in such instalments as may be required by the Stockholders or Board of Directors. In case of non-payment of any assessment or assessments on the share or shares of any Stockholder in this Company, the Directors may cause any or all such shares to be sold at public auction, and notice of every sale shall be given in one or more newspapers printed in the City of Boston, at least thirty days before the day of such sale, designating the time and place thereof. After deducting from the proceeds of sale all such assessments unpaid and interest thereon, and all charges and expenses concerning the sale, the balance of proceeds, if any, shall be paid to said delinquent Stockholder or his legal representatives.

ART. 12. These By-Laws shall not be altered except at an annual meeting, or at a special meeting of the Stockholders called for that purpose, and by a vote in which a majority of interest shall concur.

Voted, To adopt the code of By-Laws read by the Secretary, (of which the foregoing is a copy), for the government of the Corporation.

Voted, To proceed to the choice of three Directors. The Clerk was appointed to proceed and count the votes. All the votes being for Benj. L. Allen, George Odiorne, and James C. Dunn, they were declared unanimously elected.

Voted, To proceed to the choice of a Clerk and Treasurer—both offices to be filled by one person. All the votes being for William A. Hayes, he was declared unanimously elected Clerk and Treasurer of the Corporation. The Clerk was sworn to the faithful performance of his duties by Benj. L. Allen, Esq., as follows:

I, William A. Hayes, do solemnly swear that I will faithfully discharge the duties of Clerk of the Shawmut Gas Light Company—So help me God.

WILLIAM A. HAYES.

COMMONWEALTH OF MASSACHUSETTS.

Suffolk, ss. *Boston, April* 12, 1856.

Sworn before me,

B. L. ALLEN, *Justice of the Peace.*

Voted, That when this meeting adjourns it be adjourned to meet at the office of the Treasurer, on the 2d Saturday of April, 1857.

Voted, That the Clerk be, and he hereby is authorized to prepare certificates of stock and seal, and that sixty shares be issued to the proprietors of the Suffolk Gas Company, and sixty shares to the proprietors of the Shawmut Gas Light Company, as a compensation for their respective franchises.

Voted, To adjourn.

Attest: WILLIAM A. HAYES, *Secretary.*

Boston, April 12*th*, 1856.

At a meeting of the Directors of the Shawmut Gas Light Company, held at the office of J. C. Dunn, Esq., 39 State street, January 4th, 1860, — there were present Messrs. B. L. Allen, J. C. Dunn, and Geo. Odiorne.

Voted, To choose a Clerk *pro tem.* by ballot, and George Odiorne was unanimously chosen, who thereupon made and subscribed to the following oath of office, to wit:

5

SUFFOLK, SS.

I, George Odiorne, do solemnly swear faithfully to discharge and perform all the duties incumbent upon me as Clerk, *pro tem.*, of the Shawmut Gas Light Company.

GEO. ODIORNE.

Before me,

J. C. DUNN, *Justice of the Peace.*

Voted, That the President be, and he is hereby instructed, to notify the proprietors of the Company, that their annual meeting will be holden at the office of J. C. Dunn, Esq., 39 State street, Wednesday, January 18, at 10 o'clock, A. M.

Adjourned.

Attest:

GEO. ODIORNE, *Clerk, pro tem.*

[Copy of Notice printed in the Atlas and Daily Bee, January 5th, A. D. 1860.]

NOTICE.—The annual meeting of the proprietors of the Shawmut Gas Light Company will be held at the office of J. C. Dunn, No. 39 State street, Boston, on Wednesday, 18th inst., at 10 o'clock, A. M.

BENJAMIN L. ALLEN, *President.*

At a meeting of the proprietors of the Shawmut Gas Light Company, held at the office of J. C. Dunn, Esq., 39 State street, pursuant to a published notice in the Atlas and Daily Bee, of the 5th inst., calling the annual meeting of the proprietors of said Company,—

Voted, To adjourn to meet at this place at 12 M. this day.

Attest:

GEO. ODIORNE, *Clerk, pro tem.*

At a meeting of the proprietors of the Shawmut Gas Light Company, this day, January 18th, 1860, agreeably with the adjournment above, there were present Messrs. B. L. Allen, J. C. Dunn, and Geo. Odiorne.

The President, B. L. Allen, in the chair.

Voted, That Art. I. of the By-Laws be amended in the fourth line, by striking out the word "three," and substituting the word six, so that there should be six instead of three Directors; also, in the twelfth line of the same Article, by striking out the word "two," and substituting the word three, so that three Directors shall constitute a quorum.

On motion of J. C. Dunn, Esq.,—

Voted, To proceed to the choice of six Directors for the ensuing year. Whereupon the following named gentlemen were immediately elected, viz :

Benjamin L. Allen, James C. Dunn, George Odiorne, J. W. Emery, Gardiner G. Hubbard, and J. H. Converse.

Adjourned to meet again at the call of the President.

Attest :

GEO. ODIORNE, *Clerk, pro tem.*

Agreeable to the call of the President, made by sending written notice to each one of the Stockholders,—

A meeting of the Stockholders of the Shawmut Gas Light Company was holden at the office of J. C. Dunn, Esq., 39 State street, Boston, this day, at 1 o'clock in the afternoon, March 7, 1860. The President, B. L. Allen in the chair. There were present, B. L. Allen, J. C. Dunn, J. W. Emery, G. G. Hubbard, and J. H. Converse. On motion of J. H. Converse,—

Voted, That James C. Dunn, Esq., be Clerk, *pro tem.*, who there upon made oath and subscribed to the following oath of office, to wit :

Suffolk, ss.

I, James C. Dunn, do solemnly swear faithfully to discharge and perform all the duties incumbent upon me as Clerk *pro tem.* of the Shawmut Gas Light Company.

JAMES C. DUNN.

Before me,

J. M. PINKERTON, *Justice of the Peace.*

March 8th, 1860.

The draft of a contract for the construction of Gas Works for the Company having been read and duly considered, it was, on motion of J. W. Emery, Esq.,—

Voted, That the same be approved and accepted, and that the Directors of the Company be requested to execute and deliver the same on behalf of the Company.

On motion, voted to adjourn to meet at call of the President.

Attest :

JAMES C. DUNN, *Clerk, pro tem.*

The Shawmut Gas Light Company called as witnesses, Dr. Augustus A. Hayes and John H. Blake, Esq., whose testimony was as follows :

TESTIMONY OF DR. AUGUSTUS A. HAYES.

I was very well acquainted with the Boston Gas Light Company's gas, till within two years past or a little more. Was chemist for the Company till about June, 1857.

I can't now state accurately the quality of the gas, without reference to my reports, which are in the possession of the Company.

I have memoranda of my examinations at some periods : In latter part of May and first part of June, 1857.

The average quality for May, was $19\frac{1}{2}$ candles, and for June, was 18 candles, as measured by a photometer ; used Bunson's photometer ; is an accurate test ; a certain quantity of gas is consumed during the time of consumption of a candle of given weight, and the illuminating powers are thus compared.

I have memoranda of the quality in the Winter of 1856.

For December, 1856, average quality was $19\frac{1}{2}$ candles.

January, 1857, average quality was a little more than 20 candles.

The highest average whilst I was with the Company, was 22 candles ; should think for two years while I was there, the average was as high as this.

I cannot say whether it is now kept up to 22 candles. Have not lately tested it. In September last I tested the quality. It was low ; obtained no measurement over 15 candles ; cannot give the exact day. That power of illumination would indicate a low quality of gas for the Boston standard.

There are deleterious qualities in gas. The combustion of the gas has been impeded somewhat by defective purification. I have made quite a number of observations of the gas, but have no record of them. My general impression is that the illuminating power of the gas has not been maintained as high as the former standard. As nearly as I can recollect, the gas has for three years back, at the times I have examined it, been about 17 candles. This, in my judgment, is the average. There was no difficulty in keeping the gas at 22 candles, when that was the standard. When we pay for gas, we pay the same for good as for bad gas. The standard for gas in London is fixed by Act of Parliament.

The standard is 13 candles for Newcastle ; 26 candles for Cannel.

The standard in New York I do not certainly know, but I believe it is from 17 to 20 candles. Don't know the standard in Philadelphia, but a few years ago it was the same as in New York.

The deleterious quality in gas is the Carbonic Oxide in it. As I recollect the tests I have at various times made, stating merely from recollection and imperfectly, there was about 11 per cent. of Carbonic Oxide in the Boston gas previous to 1856, for three years.

I don't know their present method of purification ; have not visited the Boston Gas Works of late ; have tested the gas, and think there has been no improvement in the purification since I left. There have been great improvements made in gas manufacture, but at the period when I left their works, the most modern improvements had not been introduced. There are some small companies which use the same purification as the Boston Gas Company did — the wet purification, working the gas in lime water. The wet purification was more expensive than the dry, before the more recent improvements.

No cross examination.

James H. Blake—Gas engineer and chemist. Have built gas works ; a great many ; was employed to negotiate for land on which to erect gas works for the new company ; a negotiation has been made. A lot has been obtained in Roxbury ; a very suitable place. The land belongs to Mr. Williams and others at Roxbury Point. A new company would be beneficial in itself ; could make a profit and furnish gas at a little less than $2.25 per thousand feet ; should say at $2. Price in Philadelphia is $2.25.

The cost depends on the quantity made. I judge that the cost in Philadelphia is $2.25, including interest and payment to sinking fund ; but I get this conclusion entirely from their printed reports.

In some respects, I think a new company would benefit the old company ; it would do away with the cry of monopoly. I mean if the old company would sell out their pipes in a portion of the City to the new company. The old company has always opposed having any other company within the City proper. I have looked through the contract of the new company, for Gas Works — not with any great care ; the works proposed will be sufficient to supply the City south of Dover street.

Cross examination.

The greater the manufacture and consumption by the same company, the cheaper can it make and sell gas in proportion.

The present Gas Company is amply able to supply all prospective increase of the City of Boston. The City is none too large for it to supply perfectly. The only advantage a new company would have, would be in having entirely new Works, with all the best modern improvements. The old company to introduce them would have to disuse their old Works, which cost largely.

The price charged by the Boston Gas Company is very low ; lower than any other company that I know of, except Philadelphia.

No advantage would be gained by two companies occupying the same field, and dividing the consumers between them.

Of late years, for five or six years certainly, the aim of the Boston Gas Company has been to reduce the price of gas, rather than to increase their dividends. It reduced the price in 1852, from $3 to $2.50 and this year to $2.25.

The company did not pursue that policy formerly, I think.

The company having the whole of the City south of Dover street, could supply gas a little less than $2.25, and be a good investment.

The contract I saw was with Mr. G. G. Hubbard and Mr. J. H. Converse. It was not signed. The agreement about the land is oral.

Gas of a very high illuminating power is not, in my judgment, the best ; it is what is called a smoky gas. I don't think what is termed very rich gas is the best. It gives an intense light near at hand, but is not so diffusive a light, I think. I think the Roxbury gas better than the Boston. The Boston Company aim to have a very rich gas, and more complaints arise from the richness of the gas, than from any other cause — the gas being so highly charged with the illuminating qualities.

I think a 17 candle gas better than the high grade gases — say 22 candle gas.

If a new company had the whole field south of Dover street, I think it could sell gas at $2, and make eight per cent.

But my opinion is that as soon as the new company lays pipes in the same streets as the old company, the old company will reduce their price and the new one will do the same, and the result will be that both will be ruined.

It is not supposable that the old company will keep up its price at $2.25 with a new company selling below that price ; if it did of course the new company would get all the consumers. If the old company should put another large gas-holder at the Southwest of the City, its means of distribution would be perfect ; but that is not necessary now ; its present means are ample for all present wants. My impression is that the mains to the South End are sufficient for the present supply.

There is defective pressure in some places, because there are certain large pipes that are not connected with certain small ones, but that can be easily remedied.

I think it would be more economical for new works to be made than for the old company to extend its works at the North End.

I did at one time advise the old company to build new works at the South End; thought it would be economy for them to do so.

The evidence being closed the matter was submitted without argument.

No other evidence of any kind was offered by the Shawmut Gas Light Company, and no person residing at the South End or elsewhere, appeared to complain of an insufficient supply of gas, or of the quality or price of the gas furnished by the Boston Gas Light Company, nor advocating in any way, or desiring the establishment of a new Company. The remonstrants submit a statement of the cost of gas in the United States, published in the Boston Journal, March 12, 1860, which is believed to be accurate, and which shows that the cost of gas in Boston is as low as in any city in the United States, except Pittsburg, Pa.

THE COST OF GAS.

The announcement lately made that the price of gas was to be reduced in this City after April 1, induces us to give our readers the cost of gas in the other cities and towns in the United States, as given in John B. Murray's tables of American Gas Light Companies, corrected up to December 31, 1859, and published in the American Gas Light Journal, January 2, 1860. (New York.)

In the United States there are 334 Gas Light Companies. The price of gas per 1000 feet, as sold by these companies, is given in these tables, with the exception of 61 companies, nearly all of which are in California or in small inland towns.

The inhabitants of Auburn, Fulton, Little Falls, and Medina, N. Y., Columbus and Watertown, Ga., East Greenwich, R. I., Gunsboro, N. C., Mount Holly, N. J., St. Albans, Vt., Glaunton, Va., Belfort, Me., and Great Barrington, Mass., enjoy the luxury of gas at the modest price of $7 per 1000 feet.

In Frederick City, Md., the intensity of the light is diminished to the extent of about $4\frac{1}{2}$ per cent., and gas is sold at the rate of $6.70 per 1000 feet.

Sixteen companies sell gas at $6 per 1000 feet. Augusta, Ga., Galveston, Texas, Madison, Wis., St. Paul, Min., Woodstock, Vt., and Southbridge, Mass., are in this class. 10 sell at $5 per 1000 feet; 1, Savannah, Ga., at $4.75; 10 at $4.50; 1, Rockland, Me., at $4.80; 99 at $4; 15 at $3.80; 3 at $3.75; 9 at $3.60; 55 at $3.50; 1, Pottsville, Pa., at $3.30; 4 at $3.25; 1, Lewiston, Pa., at $3.10;

20 at $3 ; 2 at $2.70 ; 10 at $2.50 ; 1 at $2.25 ; 1, Pittsburg, Pa., at $1.50.

We give the names of the companies whose price is $3 and less ; and in order to show how far the price at which gas can be sold depends upon the extent of consumption, we give in the same columns the amount of capital stock and the number of private metres and of public lamps supplied by each of the companies.

Companies selling at $3 per 1000 feet.

	Capital.	Private. Metres.	Public Lamps.	Div's.
Akron, Ohio....................	$20,000	120	2	none
Albany, New York..............	250,000	3200	580	8 per ct.
Alleghany, Pa..................	200,000	900	200	8 "
Brooklyn, N. Y.................	2,000,000	10,000	2600	10 "
Buffalo, N. Y..................	600,000	3300	2000	10 "
Canton, Ohio..................	20,000	120	30	none.
Cleveland, Ohio...............	100,000	2000	350	10 per ct.
Columbus, Ohio...............	1,000,000	800	174	none.
Erin, Pa......................	68,000	300	80	7 per ct.
Hartford, Ct..................	175,000	1700	230	8 "
Jersey City and Hoboken........	300,000	1900	212	10 "
Johnson, Pa...................	80,000	300		6 "
Lancaster, Pa.................	100,000	620	100	8 "
Manchester, N. H..............	125,000	800	125	10 "
Massillon, Ohio	20,000	120		
Providence, R. I..............	1,000,000	4200	864	8 "
Reading, Pa...................	80,000	700	40	6 "
Rochester, N. Y...............	200,000	2100	450	10 "
Sandusky, Ohio................	75,000	300	70	
Syracuse, N. Y................	125,000	1200	272	10 "
$2.70 per 1000 feet.				
Louisville....................	$600,000	2866	951	12 per ct.
Wheeling......................	75,000	700	129	12 "
$2.50 per 1000 feet.				
Baltimore.....................	$550,000	8300	1820	10 per ct.
Boston........................	1,000,000	12,000	2265	10 "
Chicago.......................	1,300,000	4265	1100	10 "
Peoples, Chicago..............	500,000	new — no report.		
Cincinnati....................	1,000,000	6000	1700	10 "
Citizens, Brooklyn............	1,000,000	new — no report.		
Kensington, Philadelphia.......	100,000	2800	400	10 "
Northern Liberty, Philadelphia...	400,000	no report.		
New York, N. Y...............	1,000,000	13,000	3150	10 "
Manhattan, N. Y..............	4,000,000	26,000	9000	10 "
$2.25 per 1000 feet.				
Philadelphia..................	300,000	3200	5000 owned by city.	
$1.50 per 1000 feet.				
Pittsburg.....................	300,000	2624	517	10 per ct.

The cost of the coal used by this Company is $1.20 per ton of 2,000 lbs., against a price of from $5 to $12 per ton of 2,240 lbs. in the Atlantic cities.

Fredonia, N. Y., is lighted by natural gas, collected by a company having a capital of $10,000, which distributes the gas at $4.00 per thousand feet.

The average cost of gas in the United States, as gathered from this table, is $4.07 per 1,000 feet.

In the Canadas, we learn from the same tables, Halifax has gas at $3.00 per 1,000 feet; Montreal, $3.25; Quebec, $3.00; Toronto, $3.33½. Havana pays $5.00; Cardenas, $5.00.

There are several cities owning the works supplying gas. These are Alexandria, Va., price of gas, $3.50; Frankfort, Ky., $4.50; Philadelphia, Pa., $2.25; Richmond, Va., $3.80.

The Philadelphia works supply more private metres than any other company; the Manhattan Company the greatest number of public lamps. Philadelphia has 26,000 private metres; Boston has 12,000. The Manhattan supplies 9,000 public lamps; Boston has 2,265.

We give the population of the gas districts of some of the principal cities, as given in this table:—

	Pop.	Private Metres.	Pub. Lamps.	Cost.
Portland	30,000	1,900	247	$3 50
Boston	130,000	12,000	2,265	*2 25
Manhattan Co., N. Y.	600,000	26,000	9,000	2 50
New York Co., N. Y.	100,000	13,000	3,650	1 50
Brooklyn	150,000	10,000	2,600	3 00
Philadelphia	650,000	32,000	5,000	2 25
Baltimore	100,000	8,300	1,820	2 50
Washington	50,000	2,600	800	3 50
Mobile	30,000	850	200	4 50
New Orleans	120,000	5,000	2,000	4 50
Cincinnati	225,000	6,000	1,700	2 50
St. Louis	180,000	5,000	1,550	3 50
Chicago	150,000	4,265	1,100	2 50

*After April 1.

Of the companies given in these tables 164 only are reported as earning or paying dividends; 170 not paying dividends or not being reported as so doing.

The average dividends of the 164 companies reported is $8.43 per cent. per annum.

The following are all the Massachusetts Companies given:

	Capital.	Dividends.	Price per 1000 ft.
Attleboro'........................	50,000	6	$4 00
Beverly..........................	40,000		4 00
Boston 1,000,000		10	2 50
Brookline	40,000	6	3 50
Cambridge 300,000		10	3 50
Charlestown.....................150,000		8	3 50
Chelsea 100,000		7	3 50
Clinton	20,500		
Dedham	40,000		4 00
Dorchester 150,000			4 00
East Boston 133,000		8	3 50
Fall River (Private Works)........			3 50
Fitchburg.......................100,000			4 00
Gloucester.......................	40,000		3 50
Great Barrington.................	5,000		7 00
Jamaica Plains...................	50,000		
Lawrence 200,000		8	3 50
Lowell 200,000		10	3 25
Malden and Melrose..............	50,000	6	4 00
Marblehead......................	50,000		
Milford	20,000		
Nantucket	50,000	6	4 00
New Bedford....................130,000		10	3 25
Newburyport....................150,000			3 75
Newton and Watertown...........300,000		4	3 80
Northampton....................	35,000		4 00
North Bridgewater...............	50,000		
Pittsfield	40,000		4 00
Plymouth.......................	40,000	8	4 00
Roxbury........................150,000		10	3 50
Salem and South Danvers.........200,000		8	3 50
Southbridge.....................	5,000		6 00
South Boston...................200,000			3 25
Springfield.....................100,000		10	4 00
Taunton	10,000	6	4 00
Waltham........................	20,000		
Ware...........................	30,000		
West Cambridge	50,000		4 00
Worcester......................120,000		10	3 50

It is proper to say that some of these sums are given in the table as estimates only.

Thus it appears that there are in this State thirty-nine gas companies having an aggregate capital of $4,031,600, and the dividends as reported in these tables, declared by twenty companies, amount to $349,200, and the average cost of the gas as sold by the thirty-two companies whose prices are given in Murray's tables is $3.85 per 1,000 feet.

Boston alone sells gas at less than $3.25 per 1,000 feet. Lowell, and South Boston, and New Bedford sell at $3.25. Ten companies sell at $3.50, one at $3.75, one at $3.80, thirteen at $4.00, one at $6.00, and one at $7.00—of seven the price is not given.

Maine has ten companies. Capital $830,300. Six companies pay dividends averaging $7\frac{1}{2}$ per cent.

New Hampshire has five companies. Aggregate capital $330,000. Five companies pay dividends averaging $7\frac{1}{2}$ per cent.

Vermont has five companies. Aggregate capital $230,000. Only one company, Woodstock, is reported as paying dividends, and that charges $6.00 per 1,000 feet for gas.

Rhode Island has five companies. Aggregate capital $1,196,400. Four companies pay dividends, averaging $10\frac{1}{4}$ per cent.

Connecticut has nine companies. Aggregate capital $468,000. Seven companies pay dividends, averaging $8\frac{1}{7}$ per cent.

Only three of these companies charge less than $3.50 per 1,000 feet, viz: Providence, Hartford, Manchester.

Boston, as will be seen, is now, while charging $2.50 per 1000, among the lowest twelve in the United States, and after the reduction which is to take place April 1, to $2.25 per 1,000, will be surpassed in cheapness by Pittsburg only, and will have no equal except Philadelphia, where the private metres and public lamps are more than double in number than those of Boston, and are much nearer access to supplies.

It has been said, page 7, that an organization of the Suffolk Gas Company was *attempted* to be made March 21, 1856, which is entirely void, as the records themselves show.

The call for the meeting was signed " per order of the proprietors, George Odiorne," (sup. p. 27).

The statement respecting the organization of corporations in force at that time were, Rev. Statutes, ch. 44, § 3; Laws of 1855, ch. 140, § 1.

Rev. Stat. ch. 44, § 3, is as follows:—

"The first meeting of all corporations shall, unless otherwise provided for in their acts of incorporation, be called by a notice signed by any one or more of the persons named in the act of incorporation, and setting forth the time, place and purposes of the meeting; and such notice shall, at least seven days before this, be delivered to each member, or published in some newspaper of the county where the corporation may be established; or, if there be no newspaper in the county, then in some newspaper of an adjoining county; provided, that the notice of the first meeting of incorporated religious societies may be affixed to the door or some other conspicuous part of the meeting-house."

The act of 1855, ch. 140, § 1, is as follows :—

"SECT. 1. The third section of the forty-fourth chapter of the Revised Statutes is so far amended that the first meeting of all corporations shall, unless otherwise provided for in the acts of incorporation, be called by the person, or a majority of the persons, named in the act of incorporation, in the mode indicated in the said third section; and said persons so named, and their associate subscribers to stock prior to the date of their act, shall be considered the persons authorized to hold the franchise or privileges granted, until the corporation shall be organized."

It will be seen that several things are necessary to a valid call.

1. The signature of one or more of the persons named in the Act of Incorporation.

2. A statement of the time, place, and *purposes* of the meeting.

As to the first of these, it will be seen that this notice was not signed as required by law—neither of the persons named in the Act having signed the call; and it does not appear from any of the proceedings that either of the persons named in the original charter of the Suffolk Gas Company ever acted at all.

As to the second requisition, *the purposes* of the meeting must be stated.

The call set forth that the purpose of the meeting was " *to act upon the question of the acceptance of the Act of last year to unite the Suffolk and Shawmut Gas Light Companies.*" Nothing was said about accepting the original Act of Incorporation.

At the meeting the only thing done was to elect a Clerk pro tem., and Geo. Odiorne, who was not named in the charter, was elected and " qualified."

It does not appear that he was sworn.

The meeting was adjourned to March 22, 1856.

At the adjournment it was voted,—

To accept the Act of the Legislature passed April 15, 1850, incorporating the Suffolk Gas Company.

To accept the Act uniting the Shawmut and Suffolk Gas Light Companies.

This meeting was clearly unlawful. It was not called as provided by law.

The acceptance of the Act of Incorporation was void, because the only question before the meeting, if it had been lawfully called, was the acceptance of the Act of Consolidation.

From the records of the various meetings of the Suffolk Gas Company or the Shawmut Gas Light Company, it does not appear that any of the persons named in the charter of the Suffolk Gas Company were present.

The only person named in connection with the Suffolk Gas Company's meetings was George Odiorne.

No persons are stated to have been present.

No person appears to have been Chairman.

Nor does it appear that either the Shawmut Gas Light Company or the Suffolk Gas Company accepted the Act of Consolidation "at meetings *called for that purpose*, and by votes to which a majority in number and value of the proprietors in each Company shall assent," according to the requisitions of the Act.

When the meeting of the consolidated Company took place,— held on the same day, March 22, 1856, and at the same place, No. 8 Merchants Bank Building,—the records show that the usual proceedings took place.

B. L. Allen called the meeting to order. W. A. Hayes was chosen Secretary; and B. L. Allen Chairman.

From these defects, it is clear that no valid organization of the Suffolk Gas Company has ever taken place, and no valid acceptance of the Act of Consolidation of the Shawmut and Suffolk Gas Companies, and, of course, no valid consolidation of the two Corporations.

By the Statutes of 1856, ch. 264, §§ 1 and 2, the time for organization of corporations is limited.

SECT. 1. The time within which all corporations created by the General Court of this Commonwealth shall be organized, shall be limited to two years from the time of the passage of their respective acts of incorporation, except when the time is fixed in the said acts.

SECT. 2. All corporations heretofore created by the General Court, shall be authorized to organize within one year from the passage of this act, and not after; *provided*, that the term of two years since the passage of their acts of incorporation has then expired, and that there is no limitation of time in the said acts.

Under this Statute the time for organization having long since elapsed, there can now be no valid organization of the Suffolk Gas Company; and, of course, no valid consolidation of the two Corporations.

The Shawmut Gas Light Company, in pursuance of the purpose testified to before the Committee, of erecting their Works at City Point, in Roxbury, made application to the Aldermen of that City for leave to open the streets to lay pipes therein. The petition and proceedings thereon are as follows :—

To the Honorable the Mayor and Aldermen of the City of Roxbury:

The Shawmut Gas Light Company respectfully show unto your Honorable Board that they have made a conditional contract for the erection of Gas Works to supply the City of Boston with gas— the works to be located on land and wharf at the foot of Swett street, in Roxbury.

That by the Charter granted to the Suffolk Gas Light Company in 1850, they have the right to construct their works in Roxbury as well as in Boston, and to open the streets under the direction of the Mayor and Aldermen of Roxbury; that by an act passed in 1855, the Suffolk and Shawmut Gas Companies were united under the name of the Shawmut Gas Light Company, with all the rights possessed by each Company.

For the purpose of constructing their works on the land above described, your petitioners desire the privilege of laying their mains from their works through Swett and Northampton streets to the line of division between Roxbury and Boston, a distance of some five or six hundred feet.

And as in duty bound, your petitioners will ever pray.

THE SHAWMUT GAS LIGHT COMPANY,

By their Committee,

GARDINER G. HUBBARD,
JOSEPH H. CONVERSE.

A true copy of the original.

Attest: JOSEPH W. TUCKER, City Clerk.

April 2d.

Laid upon the table.

May 7th, 1860.

IN BOARD OF ALDERMEN.

Taken from the table, and ordered that the petitioners have leave to withdraw their petition.

(Signed,)   JOSEPH W. TUCKER, City Clerk.

From these proceedings it appears that the purpose of the Shawmut Gas Light Company to erect Works out of the City cannot now be carried into effect.

It will be also observed that the power of this Corporation to erect its Works in Roxbury, depends upon the extent of the charter of the Suffolk Gas Light Company, which alone had authority to go into Roxbury. This charter being, as has been shown, void, it never having been legally organized, no right exists in any existing Gas Company to erect Works in Roxbury.

The subscribers hereto, in behalf of themselves and the other remonstrants, now before your Honorable Board, therefore urge that the Order passed July 18, 1854, authorizing the streets to be opened to lay gas pipes, be rescinded.

1. Because the laying of two sets of gas pipes in the streets will subject the citizens to great and unnecessary inconvenience, inasmuch as

2. The South End is now well supplied with gas of good quality, and at a low price.

3. Because the Shawmut Gas Light Company has never been legally consolidated with the Suffolk Gas Light Company,

and, inasmuch as the Suffolk Gas Light Company has never been duly or legally organized, and the space of two years has elapsed since its charter was granted, never can be.

4. Because if the City permits its streets to be opened by a Gas Company not properly organized, it will be liable for all damages which may accrue to individuals arising from such opening or use of the streets.

LEOPOLD HERMAN,
CHARLES ROLLINS,
FRANCIS BOYD,
WILLIAM PARKMAN,
ALDEN SPEARE,
SYLVESTER BOWMAN,
CHARLES S. KENDALL,
WM. W. CLAPP, Jr.,
A. A. RANNEY,
R. W. BURKE,
F. W. SAWYER,
N. C. POOR,
TOLMAN WILLEY,
E. GERRY DUDLEY.

HARVEY JEWELL, *Of Counsel*
JOHN S. HOLMES, *for the*
H. W. SUTER, *Remonstrants.*

www.ingramcontent.com/pod-product-compliance
Lightning Source LLC
Chambersburg PA
CBHW030722110426
42739CB00030B/1201